# Invocations for Beginners

## Calling upon a Deity:
## A Foundation of Magic

for Naropa

**Contact:**  www.HarryEilenstein.de
Harry.Eilenstein@web.de
Harry Eilenstein at youtube

**Production and publishing:**  BoD  -  Books on Demand, Norderstedt

**ISBN:**  9783753454351

# Table of Contents

# I  What is an Invocation?

An invocation is simply the (usually temporary) identification with a deity. The word "invocation" means "calling in." So one invokes a deity into oneself, with whom one then identifies.

This sounds a bit like deliberate megalomania, but the concrete experience of an invocation is clearly different from megalomania.

Every prayer to a deity, every talisman dedicated to a deity, every meditation on a deity, every trust in a deity is a small invocation, a step on the way to an invocation: one approaches a deity and seeks a connection to it.

Invocations are found in all religions, although the methods for achieving "intimate connection with a deity" are different:

> In the Christian Jesuit order, each monk reads the New Testament daily according to the instructions of the order's founder, Igantius of Loyola. In doing so, however, the monk does not assume the attitude of an outside observer, but always the position of Christ: he reads and experiences every situation from Christ's point of view. In this way, he increasingly suffuses and identifies himself with Christ.

> In Jewish mysticism, one strives for identification with Yahweh or with Adam Kadmon, who is the perfect man united with God. An important element in this is understanding and meditation.

> In Islam and Islamic mysticism (Sufism), this identification is achieved primarily through love of Allah.

> In Hinduism, there is a great variety of meditations, rituals and cults to achieve this attachment to a deity.

> In Buddhism, mandalas, meditations and rituals are used to gradually become like Buddha.

> Invocations also exist in the lesser known, smaller religions, although they seem to be less common there.

> Invocation is primarily an element of monotheistic religions: God is the source of the world, the king is the controller of the realm, the ego is the center of man, truth is the core of philosophy – in the worldview of monotheism there is always an original unity from which the diversity of

creation emanates. Therefore, every form of self-knowledge and every form of self-expression is based on the return to this original center – and ultimately, therefore, on the return to God, to the invocation of God, in the unity with God.

The invocation of a deity still originates from shamanism: one of the main tasks of shamans was and is to call the spirits of the deceased to their still living descendants, so that they may assist them with advice and help. In the early Neolithic period (10,500-8,500 B.C.), the ancestral spirits were called into their skulls; then in the middle Neolithic period (8,500-5,000 B.C.) into their skulls, which were covered with clay and plasticized into as lifelike a portrait head of the deceased as possible; and then finally (5000-3250 B.C.) into a stone statue of the deceased. These three Neolithic phases were not sharply demarcated from each other, but flowed smoothly into each other.

The statues were obviously something like a "second body" for the soul of the dead person, which gradually developed from the skull of the dead person.

Then, as the archetype of the mother, various mythological motifs, and some ancestors evolved into deities during the Neolithic period, statues were also made as secondary bodies for these deities.

At first, these statues were simply a shaped piece of wood, clay or stone. Only by the shaman calling the spirit of the dead person or the deity into a statue, this shaped piece of wood, clay or stone became an "inhabited statue".

In various forms of magic, the magician identified with other beings already in the Paleolithic Age – the identification with the panther can be traced back the longest by the hunters, who wanted to be able to hunt as effectively as a panther (late Paleolithic Age). So the oldest known invocations were animal invocations.

It was obvious to connect these animal invocations with the calling in of the ancestors and deities into their statues: In this way, the invocation of an ancestor into one's own body (family constellations) or of a deity into one's own body (invocation) came into being.

The method, which is known today as "systemic family constellations", originated from South African shamans, who used this invocation variant to establish contact with the ancestors.

The principle of identification is still widespread today: Almost every young person has a role model, an ideal, of which he has a poster hanging on his room wall …

The successful, lasting invocation is described in many religions in the same way: Man becomes a child of the deity in question. This invocation and permanent connection is found in yogis, saints, founders of religions, kings, etc.

This "child of a deity" motif is found, for example, in the ancient Egyptian pharaoh who called himself "Son of the Sun," in the Chinese emperor who was called "Son of

Heaven," in the Inca (king of the Qetchua Indians) who was addressed as "Son of the Sun," in Christ who is known as "Son of God," etc.

On the way to the successful invocation with a deity, one often finds several steps that build on each other:

| | |
|---|---|
| 1st stage: | waking consciousness, body consciousness |
| 2nd step: | experiencing the power animal, the power plant and the power stone |
| 3rd step: | experiencing one's own soul |
| 4th step: | invocation of a deity |
| 5th step: | unity with the one God |

These five stages are a gradual expansion of one's consciousness to more and more comprehensive areas.

These five stages correspond to the "Middle Pillar" from the Kabbalah. From it is derived a meditation called "Exercise of the Middle Pillar" which is the short form of a comprehensive invocation. It will be described in more detail later.

# II  The Use of the Invocation of a Deity

According to the descriptions given so far, an Invocation seems to be something quite extraordinary and strenuous – at least if you do it purposefully, systematically and with great commitment and do not just pin a poster of your own youth idol on the wall of your room. Therefore, the legitimate question arises as to the benefit of such an invocation.

Well – if the Invocation is what it promises to be, one's own waking consciousness unites with the consciousness of a deity and consequently with the possibilities of perception and action of a deity. Since the possibilities of a deity go far beyond the possibilities of a human being, one expands also ons's own possibilities by an invocation.

One can assume that the experience of this expansion will be quite uniform in itself, but that the concrete experiences will depend very much on the particular deity invoked. Depending on the special request one has, one will invoke different deities. This expansion of one's possibilities through an invocation allows one's "ordinary magic" to become "extraordinary magic."

The greatest gift of an invocation, however, is the experience of dissolving the boundaries of one's own consciousness: a deity has a clearly defined character, but no boundaries – it is everywhere at once. One can reach this state through an invocation, among other things.

Naturally, one can point to this experience with words and one can also describe the individual steps by which one can get there – but the experience itself cannot be described by words in such a way that one can experience it. You have to experience the experience yourself – only then can you really understand what is meant by the words that describe it.

It is worth it.

# III  The Choice of the Deity

Which deity should one invoke? As a rule, this question does not really arise.

Most of the time, you have a concrete goal that you want to achieve with the help of magic – then the invoked deity results from this goal.

Or one has always had an inclination to a certain deity – to a deity who has a similar character as oneself … With some probability this will be one's own protective deity, i.e. the deity of whose "sea" one's own soul is a "drop".

In the case that one has decided to invoke ons's own protective deity, one can ask oneself whether one has chosen the deity or rather the deity has chosen one. Probably the closest to reality is to assume that both have chosen each other.

Of course, a human being can't only worship one deity in his life. A dedicated magician or a curious witch will try out many possibilities and experience many things – but as a rule one comes back to one's own protective deity and invokes it most often, because it corresponds best to one's own character and one feels most at home with it and this deity has exactly the characteristics and abilities one is looking for.

So there is a free choice of the deity, but in reality this choice is a gradual approach to what is already there: the connection to one's own protective deity.

# IV   Getting to Know the Deity

The first step of an invocation is usually getting to know the deity. One can, of course, base an invocation only on the name of a deity and just call it into oneself, but this adventure-oriented approach will be rather rare – perhaps with a magician with a Uranus/Neptune conjunction on the Ascendant that has a sextile to Pluto …

## IV 1.   Study

In order to be able to invoke a deity, one must first know that it exists – this will be done in most cases by reading something about it. If you are curious about it, you will probably look for more texts about it and probably also for old hymns to it, myths that have been passed down, mentions of it in legends, and so on. If one is lucky, there is also a book about the deity in which all known texts about this deity have already been collected.

Possibly there are also pictures of the deity – preferably from the time when the deity was still generally worshipped in a culture. Possibly statues of the deity can be found or even whole temples. If the deity is very important to you, you might even plan your vacation so that you can visit a temple of that deity. Sometimes, however, you can find ancient statues of the deity already in the ethnological museum of the nearest big city.

If you want to be especially thorough, you can also try to reconstruct the history of this deity – even deities have a biography and change over time.

You can go to any length, if you will: In order to understand Osiris better, I studied the old Egytian languge.

An important and revealing aspect is also the connection of the selected deity to other deities, so ultimately the entire mythology of which this deity is a part. One can always understand a deity only as a part of a larger whole …

A very important element in getting to know a deity are also conversations with other people who have already had experiences with the deity in question.

# IV 2.  Dream Journeys

In addition to the "normal method" just described for gaining knowledge about a subject, there is also the "direct method" of dream travel.

In dream travel, one is in a state of consciousness in which the waking consciousness has been coordinated and integrated with the dream state, i.e., with the subconscious. Thus one is fully awake in one's subconsciousness and can "dream" awake and purposefully – hence the term "dream journey".

This state is generally known, but has not yet been firmly inserted into our culture as a normal possibility of action: It is the state in the morning immediately after awakening, when one continues to dream for five seconds and the dream still maintains its own independent momentum – or the state when one has had a vivid daydream on the train ride and has again felt the sand under one's feet on one's last beach vacation.

The dream journey has a great advantage: telepathy is the "eyes" of the subconscious mind – just as telekinesis is the "hand" of the subconscious mind. Therefore, on a dream journey it is much easier than in the waking state to obtain information in a telepathic way.

On a dream journey one can not only explore what is in one's own psyche, but also by telepathy the healing effect of a plant, the place where the lost front door key is, or even the character of a deity.

On a dream journey one can travel to a deity and talk to it or ask it for advice and help. In the process, the deity itself is quite active and sometimes says and does things that you did not expect at all. Possibly the deity is also of the opinion that for its visitor completely different things are important than those, which the visitor itself considers important … Dream journeys, on which nothing happens, that one did not expect at all, are extremely rare.

Dream journeys not only expand one's knowledge of a deity, but also create a personal contact with the deity – the deity becomes real in a way that can never be brought about by mere study. It is simply something different to converse with a deity "live" than to merely read something about it …

# IV 3.  Art

Depending on one's own disposition, one may get the impulse to paint the deity.

You might also write some verses about her, or a hymn to the deity, or write a myth about the deity yourself.

If you are more of a "hand" type, you could also sculpt a statue of the deity, mold it out of clay or plasticine, carve it out of soapstone or wood, cast it out of bronze, or even carve it out of stone, grind and polish it.

You may also be more of a musician and compose a song or small sonata for the deity. Possibly one will improvise music – for example, playing on a pan flute for Pan, on a lyre for Apollo, on a harp for Bragi or Dagda, or on a drum for the earth goddess.

Another possibility is the dance. There are traditional dances to deities such as the Indian temple dance to Shiva, the Thai Buddha dances, the African and Indian Sun dances, the many war dances among different peoples, and so on.

As an architect, one might have the idea to build a model of a temple for this deity or to create a stone circle in which this deity is then worshipped.

Finally, there is also the possibility of the play, which represents the myths of the deity – which is already very close to the mystery plays.

There are hardly any limits to the artistic possibilities of approaching a deity.

# IV 4.  Kabbalah

In the Kabbalah there is the symbol of the Tree of Life, which represents a structure that is contained in all things in the world and from which, among other things, the Tarot cards are derived.

On this tree of life a snake crawls up, which represents the way from the everyday consciousness to God and thus also embodies the coming to know of a deity. This path is represented in the Tarot by the "Major Arcana" from the "Fool" to the "World". This is the "path of knowledge". This "serpent of wisdom" is also the Kundalini. This serpent is a helper in the invocation.

A second symbol on the Tree of Life is the Lightning Ray of Creation, which represents the path from God to the mundane world. This path is represented in the Tarot by the "Minor Arcana" – from the four "1" cards to the four "10" cards. This is the "path of creation." It's the deity that comes in answer to the invocation: One rises first like the Kundalini-Serpent – then the deity decends like a lightning flash.

A third symbol on the Tree of Life is the "Middle Pillar" which represents the five essential levels: the body, the power animal, the soul, the guardian deity and God.

One does not have to know Kabbalah to be able to invoke a deity, but the Kabbalistic Tree of Life can help one gain an orientation to the processes involved in invocation.

# V  The Connection to the Deity

Now that one has gained an overview of the traditional ideas about the chosen deity through study, and has subsequently established a personal relationship with the deity through dream journeys, artistic representations, and the like, one can now further develop and strengthen the connection to the deity.

Here again there are a variety of possibilities.

## V 1.  Mantra and Chant

The simplest method is to use the name of the deity as a mantra. The simplest variation of using a mantra is again to inwardly chant the name of the deity once while inhaling and once while exhaling.

An addition to this would be to imagine (while inwardly speaking the name) inhaling life force and directing it to the heart chakra. Then, while exhaling (and inwardly speaking the name), imagine that the life force is shining in the heart chakra. This can be done as a meditation, but also while walking, riding a bicycle, working, etc.

Another addition to the simple mantra would be a melody to the name, which may be spoken several times. For some deities there are such melody mantras in the tradition.

The inwardly chanted mantra then leads to the outwardly chanted mantra. It is especially effective to chant such a mantra together in a group.

It is most effective and therefore also most meaningful to perform this chanting in a meditative setting, but there is also the possibility to let such a spoken or chanted mantra run along inwardly with everything one does and to possibly speak or chant it outwardly as well. This can be done in any situation, but if you are a saleswoman in a bakery, for example, you should be careful where and when the external chanting of the mantra is appropriate and when it is not …

# V 2.  Temple and Cult

A daily or at least regular cult in a proper temple of the chosen deity is possible only in a few cases – in this country especially if this deity is Christ, Mary, Allah or possibly Yahweh.

However, one can certainly build an altar in one's own four walls and possibly also set up a meditation corner. If you earn enough money, you can even set up a whole room as a temple.

If you know some like-minded people, there is also the possibility to afford such a temple room together. Of course, this is easiest in connection with a sect, a magical order, a witch coven or any other magical or religious community.

Possibly you can also choose a clearing in the forest or a similar place near your home for your rituals. For everyday use, however, a small "meditation rug" in one's living room as a "temple" is most practical.

Also the cult does not necessarily have to be very elaborate – one can also start with lighting an incense stick in front of the statue of a deity.

By "cult" is meant that one gives an outer form to one's own invocation of a deity, i.e. a place reserved for this purpose, a statue of the deity, some incense sticks, a vase for flowers, etc. – just what one used to call a "house altar".

If one looks for the suitable place for this house altar, one needs only to look around where the television or the wide screen is – it has taken over the former place of the house altar in almost all households …

# V 3. Imagination

The most important tool in the invocation is the imagination, i.e. the creation of the most vivid, colorful and three-dimensional inner image of the deity. Again, there are different approaches.

 - One can look at an image of the deity, then close one's eyes and recall this image.

 - One can look at a statue of the deity, then close the eyes and recall this image internally.

 - One can paint an image of the deity or sculpt a statue of the deity oneself based on the images and statues one knows. This can make the subsequent imagining of the figure of the deity much easier.

 - One can make dream journeys to the deity and then contemplate it – its face, facial expressions, shape, clothing, symbols, gestures, the sound of its voice, its character reflected in its face, and so on.

By contemplating this inner image of the deity, a memory image of the deity arises in one, which one can then in most cases quite easily imagine even outside the dream journey.

One can practice imagining the deity in three stages:

 - first seeing the deity on a dream journey,

 - then imagining the deity outside a dream journey with closed eyes,

 - and finally imagining the deity with open eyes, i.e. at a place in the room where one is.

Ideally, with eyes open, one has the impression that the deity in question is standing in front of one in the room – in the consistence of "dense vapors." When you then look into the eyes of the deity and feel that you are also being looked at by it, then the imagination has really come alive.

In order to successfully perform an invocation, such an intense imagination is very helpful, but not absolutely necessary.

It is useful to consider in which way one can learn the imagination most easily:

- through the imagination of a symbol,
- by imagining symbols, angels, etc. in a ritual,
- through dream journeys,
- through the contemplation of a statue of a god,
- by imagining a deity while chanting a song to that deity, etc.
  etc.

There is almost always one method that one finds significantly easier than all other methods – this seems to be dream journeys in most cases.

# V 4. Use

Just as a muscle becomes stronger when you use it, the connection to a deity also becomes stronger when you use it – moreover, you get to know the deity better and better in the process and thus also become more familiar with it.

- This "using the deity" can be occasional requests to it, which can range from a wish for a parking space in the city crowded with cars to a wish for a relationship and healing from a serious illness. You can calmly ask for anything, even if, according to the myths of the deity, it is not within its traditional competence. You will see what happens …

- Conversations with the deity are also very beneficial. This does not necessarily mean conversations on a dream journey, but also questions on the sideline while sitting in the subway. You can ask about everything and then see what you get as an answer. In this way one gets to know the deity and its views and abilities better and better.

- Finally, one can ask the deity to appear in one's consciousness as a warning intuition in critical situations – that is, in situations where one overlooks something essential, where one is about to do something that one would later regret, where one fails to recognize a danger, etc.

Deities very rarely speak up on their own – probably because they respect people's personal freedom. However, if you make a cooperation agreement with them, so to speak, and tell them when you would be glad to have them intervene on what your doing, you open a gate through which abundant advice and help can then flow to you from the deity in question.

Since one seeks with large probability only then a more intensive contact to a deity, if one has a similar character as this deity (which is possibly even the own protection deity), one' own wishes and the wishes of this deity to a large extent are the same. By making a cooperation agreement with the deity, you allow the deity to do in the magician's life what the deity would most like to do there anyway.

One pulls on the same rope, one goes in the same direction …

These are three starting points for the use of the connection with the Deity, but there are, of course, many more variations and shades of this use, ranging from simple prayer to the miraculous deeds of Christ, some saints, some yogis and other magic specialists.

# V 5.  Transmission of Consciousness

A very simple and at the same time very effective method of getting to know someone can be tried on a dream journey: changing with one's own consciousness into a deity. This can also be considered as "invocation on a dream journey".

The procedure is very simple: when you see the deity in front of you, you ask it if it would be all right for you to cross over into it with your own consciousness. If the deity agrees, you then do that – you go, so to speak, into the deity.

One can then also look at various myths of these deities from the deity perspective – there are no limits to creativity. Often the myths also become much more tangible and understandable through this "experiencing from the deity's perspective". This is the method that is used by the Jesuit monks: they read the New Testament from the perspective of Christ.


# V 6.  Umbilical Cord

It may be helpful to imagine an umbilical cord from oneself to the deity. The umbilical cord is the archetype of the connection to another being.

You can imagine this umbilical cord yourself or ask the deity to create it. It often runs from one's own navel to the navel of the god or to the womb of the goddess.

One should simply see how such an umbilical cord feels to oneself, and then decide if one wants to expand this imgaination and use it in other contexts – e.g. when one calls the deity, when one needs help from it, when one performs a ritual addressed to it, etc.

Again, as almost everywhere in magic, there are general rules, but you should apply each rule in your own style so that you can use the rule effectively.

# V 7.   The Horoscope

As in all of "normal life," one's horoscope has an effect everywhere in magic. The horoscope can help to grasp one's own style and also to see how to proceed most sensibly in an invocation. The following are just a few brief suggestions, as a complete astrological description of the various approaches to performing an invocation would fill an entire book.

The most formative is the Ascendant:

- Aries Ascendant: Invocation is done spontaneously, when one feels like it or when circumstances require it. Long preparations are avoided.

- Taurus-Ascendant: The thing must be tangible, one must be able to see the benefit, one wants to be able to touch the deity and therefore looks for a statue of it. It would be advantageous if it were a deity of enjoyment.

- Gemini Ascendant: You just try different methods and see what happens. Going the same way every time is rather boring and ineffective – the new increases concentration and therefore effectiveness.

- Cancer Ascendant: You can only invoke a deity that you feel belongs to your kinship. You approach it gradually and see how much trust you have in it, and thereby determine what distance you need from it and how much closeness you can allow.

- Leo Ascendant: You do it the way you want to do it – and it is important that it is a deity that promotes individuality, egocentricity, will and self-realization.

- Virgo Ascendant: The deity is carefully researched in all details, the invocation precisely planned and all contingencies thought out beforehand. It should also be a deity of order.

- Libra Ascendant: The harmonious overall impression is important, the beauty of the texts, the evenness of the statue, the uniform style of the tempel, etc. Music would also be beneficial. Deities of beauty and rightness are preferred. Invocation is establishing harmony with a deity, a conversation and friendship with it.

- <u>Scorpio Ascendant</u>: Invocations are conceived as an ecstatic process – a heightening is sought that dissolves the old forms and creates new ones. Gods of dance and intoxication are preferred.

- <u>Sagittarius-Ascendant</u>: The invocation succeeds best when a great goal is aimed at with it – the deity is the helper on the way to this goal.

- <u>Capricorn Ascendant</u>: One trusts an invocation text only if it is old and tested and if its authenticity has been proved. One looks to see who is the greatest authority in the field of invocations and then follows his instructions.

- <u>Aquarius Ascendant</u>: One always sees a deity against the background of the whole mythology – and one sees a deity as an image within the Great Whole, which is what it is really all about. The deity is, so to speak, a letter in the world formula, which one wants to grasp in the end – for which one first tries to understand the "letter" of this deity.

- <u>Pisces-Ascendant</u>: One feels into the Godhead, one opens oneself to it and resonates with it. The important thing is that you feel attracted to it – when the "wind of the deity" blows in the direction in which you want to sail your sailing ship, you open yourself to it.

The imprint of the Ascendant is complemented by the planets in the 1$^{st}$ house, which begins with the Ascendant:

- <u>Moon in the 1$^{st}$ house</u>: For the Moon, the images and moods of the deity are the most important.
  Maternal deities are preferred.

- <u>Mercury in the 1$^{st}$ house</u>: For Mercury the invocations and the myths are the most important.
  Wisdom deities and cunning deities are preferred.

- <u>Venus in the 1$^{st}$ house</u>: For Venus, affection, love for the deity is the most important thing.
  Erotic deities are preferred.

- <u>Sun in 1$^{st}$ house</u>: For the Sun, the most important thing is the connection with a greater radiance that unites with one's own radiance.
  Deities that form the center of a mythology are preferred.

21

- <u>Mars in the 1<sup>st</sup> house</u>: For Mars, the actions in the invocation are the most important.
   Warlike ecstatic deities are preferred.

   - <u>Jupiter in the 1<sup>st</sup> house</u>: For Jupiter the clear orientation and the contradiction-free goal are the most important.
   Fathers of the gods, deities of wealth, and the like are preferred.

   - <u>Saturn in the 1<sup>st</sup> house</u>: For Saturn, the clear, unambiguous form of ritual and procedure is the most important thing.
   Primal deities are preferred.

   - <u>Uranus in the 1<sup>st</sup> house</u>: For Uranus, spontaneity is the most important thing – and that there is something new.
   Deities of invention and chaos are preferred.

   - <u>Neptune in the 1<sup>st</sup> house</u>: For Neptune, boundary-dissolving empathy is the most important thing.
   Deities of vastness such as sea gods are preferred.

   - <u>Pluto in the 1<sup>st</sup> House</u>: For Pluto, the intensity of both motivation and execution and experience is the most important thing.
   Deities of the underworld and of transformation are preferred.

# VI  The Invocation of the Deity

In principle, an invocation is very simple: one imagines the deity as vividly and colorfully as possible a few steps in front of oneself in space and then goes to that place and identifies with the deity there.

However, since this is usually an unfamiliar process, many tools and variations have been developed for this purpose.

One can perform an invocation quite simply by doing only the most necessary: imagining the deity, then going to it and identifying oneself with this image of the deity.

However, one can also make a ritual out of the invocation that makes this imagining of the deity and identification with it easier. The following is a selection of tools. Which and how many of these aids one should use, one cannot say generally – that is different for everyone again. It therefore makes sense to start with a simple variant and then expand it step by step and see what works well for you and what does not.

There is also a general dynamic: most of the time you start with a simple ritual variant, which then gradually becomes more and more complex, but then after some time becomes simpler again, until finally you don't need a ritual at all for the Invocation.

A ritual is an aid to imagination and concentration and as such very useful, but not absolutely necessary.

At first, too many details would tend to confuse, but with time, one can create an overall image of the deity, so to speak, in the ritual. When this image has come alive in oneself, small hints about the different aspects of the deity will eventually suffice. Then, when one has become familiar with the deity, one needs fewer and fewer aids – until one can finally perform such an invocation while standing in line at the checkout in the supermarket – no one notices anything about what one is doing inwardly.

# VI 1.   The Place of the Ritual

## VI 1. a)   The Place

For some invocations there are particularly well-suited places. If you have such a place within reach, you should try an invocation of the deity to which this place fits. Such places can be quite different:

- a sweat lodge for the mother goddess,
- a stone circle for a sun god,
- an island for an otherworldly deity,
- a mountain for a father god,
- a coast for a sea god,
- a forest for wilderness deities
- a cemetery for deities of transformation,
- a cave for an underworld deity,
- a church for Christ,
- a mosque for Allah,
- an Indian temple for a Hindu deity,
  etc.

## VI 1. b)   The Room

One can also decorate the room where one is going to perform the Invocation according to the deity:

- with pictures and statues of the deity,
- with cloths in a color that matches the deity,
- with images of deities that appear in the myths of the chosen deity,
- a carpet symbolizing the "consecrated place",
  etc.

# VI 2.  The Ritual Clothing

## VI 2. a)  The Clothing

One can also dress in a special way. The simplest way is a shirt and trousers or a dress, which one wears only during rituals. This is definitely an aid to concentration that should not be underestimated.

You can also sew a long robe that you wear only during rituals – you should do what feels good for you.

A more elaborate method would be to make clothes and symbols that fit the deity and that you gradually put on and hold in your hand during the invocation. This is especially a variant for people who like to have all magical-spiritual things "tangible", as well as for group rituals, where everything that is visible makes the coordination of concentration and imagination in the group much easier.

The same as for clothes goes for jewellery.

## VI 2. b)  The Symbols

One may, in addition to the "special clothing", use various objects during the invocation such as a wand, an ankh (life force symbol), a flute, a cross, a chalice, etc.

The use of such symbolic objects should be based on what one finds helpful. A little experimentation is extremely helpful here, as with most things, for nothing creates a better fundament than one's own concrete experience.

# VI 3.   The Statue

## VI 3. a)   The Incense

A widely used tool is incense, which goes back to the burnt offering. The original idea is that the burning incense releases life force that is transferred to the statue. The life force in the statue then invites the deity to enter that statue.

Therefore, the Egyptians called the incense "Se-netjer", i.e. "that which makes divine".

In addition to this magical aspect of incense, there is also the fact that the sense of smell, unlike the other senses, is connected to the cerebellum and not to the cerebrum, and consequently causes instinctive reactions. As a result, smells immediately create associations with previous situations in which one smelled the same thing. Consequently, if one always burns the same incense during all rituals or invocations, one awakens memories of earlier rituals in oneself just by burning this incense.

You can also use these associations in a more sophisticated way by using an incense mixture for each deity that you do not use for anything else. In this way, one can establish a basic concentration on the deity simply by burning incense.

## VI 3. b)   The Statue

A statue of the deity standing in front of one on a pedestal, table or the like can be a great aid to imagination. First of all, you can imagine that the deity takes the statue as its "second body" – the deity is then in front of you in the statue. In a second step, one can then imagine how the deity comes out of the statue to oneself and completely fills and envelops oneself.

Instead of a statue, one can also use an image of the deity.

Both the statue and the image need not be large, but if they are large, they are naturally more impressive, which facilitates the imagination.

## VI 3. c)  Decorating the Statue

If you look at ancient rituals that were performed in temples, you will see that the statues were treated like human beings: They were washed, oiled and dressed in the morning, their crowns, necklaces and bracelets were put on them, they were given food and drink and talked to. This custom can be found in cultures as diverse as the ancient Egyptians and the Germanic tribes.

These elements can be included in an invocation – they facilitate the imagination that a deity is present in the statue.


## VI 3. d) The Sacrifice

The offering has the same function as the incense: the life force that is in the offering is transferred to the statue. Originally, the life force from the sacrifice was the food for the spirit of the dead or for the deity in the statue.

In the beginning, the offerings were killed, burned, broken or destroyed in some other way so that they were "dead" and consequently could pass into the afterlife to the ancestral spirit.

Later, the offerings were merely handed to the spirit of the dead or the deity in the statue, who then took the life force from the offering. Afterwards, the food and drink could then be consumed by the people.

The same is correspondingly true of offerings consisting of flowers, jewelry, and the like.

It is obvious, though not absolutely necessary, to select offerings that are appropriate to the deity one wishes to invoke.

# VI 4.   The Invocation

## VI 4. a)   The Foundation

One can begin the invocation immediately – but one can also lead the ritual gradually toward the invocation. For example, a ritual structure could look like this:

     1. A protection ritual for the place (drawing a circle, pentagram ritual or similar).

     2. State aloud what you are going to do.

     3. Call in the four directions the element, which fits to the deity (possibly with the element-pentagrams).

     4. Invoke the planet in the four directions that corresponds to the deity (possibly with the planet hexagrams).

     5. Invoke the deity.

     6. Conclusion.

## VI 4. b)   The Invocation

The invocation, i.e. the words that are spoken, are often the central part of an invocation. One can speak them aloud or just inwardly. If you are doing the invocation in pairs or as a group, speaking aloud makes more sense because then everyone knows what is happening. The words of the invocation describe the deity being invoked on the one hand and what is happening on the other.

In the beginning, one will probably prefer to use already existing invocations, i.e. to read them aloud during the invocation. One may also memorize the text in order to be freer in the ritual. Next, one will probably compose invocations that correspond more precisely to one's own ideas about the deity. Finally, one will proceed to improvise these invocations. At least this is a widespread dynamic ...

The invocations usually have five phases, which can be clearly distinguished:

1st phase: First, the invocation describes the appearance of the deity. Various epithets of the deity are used.

In this phase, one speaks about the deity in the 3rd person: "She is …"; "She is called …"; "She does …" etc.

One looks at the deity still distanced – this is the phase of the imagination.

2nd phase: Now the relations, the symbols, the temples etc. of the deity are described. The different relations of the deity to other deities play a role.

In this phase one speaks about the deity in the 2nd person: "You are …"; "You are called …"; "You do …" etc.

One speaks with the deity and establishes a connection with it – an exchange takes place, life force flows from the deity to the invoker, an umbilical cord is formed between the deity and the invoker.

3rd phase: Now the previous deeds and the general goals of the deity are described. In particular, the deeds and goals because of which one wants to invoke this deity are emphasized.

In this phase, one speaks about the deity in the 1st person: "I am …"; "My name is …"; "I do …" etc.

One speaks as the deity – one has united with the imagined image of the Deity and has identified oneself with the deity.

4th phase: the character of this phase depends on the reason for the invocation:

> - If one simply wants to experience the deity, one now feels the deity, speaks as the deity, moves as the deity, dances as the deity – whatever comes to mind in this state.

> - If one has had a very concrete wish for the deity, such as a healing, then one will now heal the illness in question as the deity – by gradually shrinking the illness, by taking the illness out of the body, by imagining the healed state, and so on.

> - If one has a desire related to the myths of the deity, then one will now enter and experience this mythe as a deity.
> Someone who has Osiris as a patron deity is likely to experience constant cyclical profound transformations in their life. The person

might then enter into the myth in which Osiris is killed by Seth and reborn by Isis to better understand this myth and its dynamics and thus his own life.

5<sup>th</sup> phase: When the previous phase is completed, there are two possibilities:

    - One gradually leaves the image of the deity, returns to oneself and thanks the deity for the experience.

    - However, one can also remain in the image of the deity and let this connection continue to exist as a semi-conscious background. This is especially obvious if one has invoked one's own protective deity, with whom one is constantly connected through one's soul anyway.
    But also if you want to have e.g. the power of Ares, the organizing talent of Jupiter or the seductive arts of Pan permanently in your life, you can simply end the invocation with a silent fading out of the ritual without dissolving the connection to the deity.

The structure of the invocation text has been described here in great detail, but not in every successful invocation such a text has been used. The main purpose of this detailed description is to make clear the principle of step-by-step imagination and identification and to show as many tools and procedures as possible for writing an invocation text.

There is also the possibility to invoke a deity completely formless and to be successful with it. The point is not to use the most carefully polished invocation of the deity, but to experience oneself as the deity. To achieve this goal, one should use the methods that work best for oneself.

The three steps of the actual invocation („He is …", „You are …", and „I am …") are the common steps of an integration: „to see, to feel, and to embrace". These steps are also found in psychic healing processes. They can also be descibed as „perception, contact, and integration".

# VI 4. c)   The Mandala

A mandala is a magical-spiritual map. The simplest mandala is the division of the world into the material world, the otherworld, and the boundary between both. Such simple mandalas are often painted by the shamans on the skin of their drums – supplemented by the images of the beings and things they have seen on their afterlife journeys.

The more complex mandalas often consist of several concentric circles and a cross that divides these circles into quarter circles.

**Example of a simple Mandala**

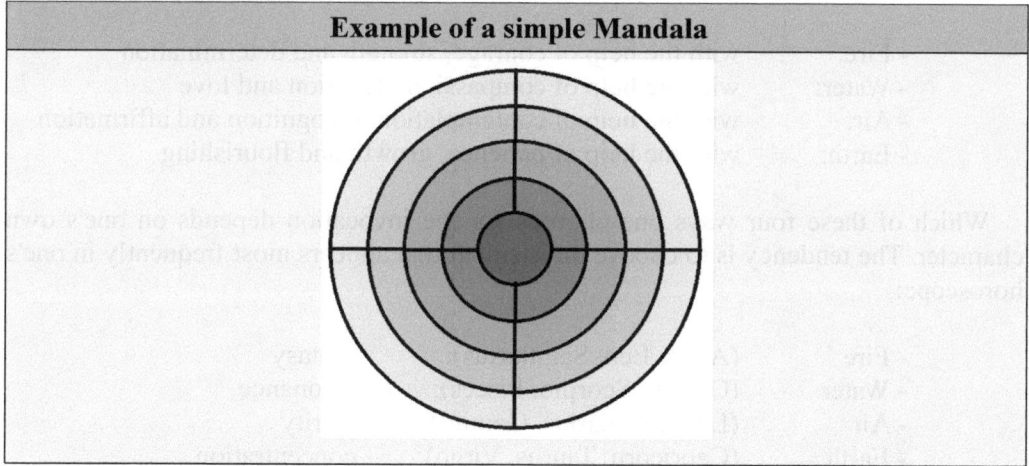

From the inside out, these circles or circular rings can have the following meaning, for example:

- circle in the center               = One God, central deity
- innermost circle ring              = deities in the continuum
- second innermost circular ring    = soul in the beyond (soul realm)
- second outermost circle ring       = power animal in the realm of life force
- outermost circular ring           = body in the material world

The way from the outermost circle ring to the inner circle is thus a way from the everyday consciousness in the material body to a deity. This means that the way into the center of a mandala is also a gradual invocation (the way leads from the bottom to the top in the following list):

31

| | |
|---|---|
| - circle in the center | = unity with the deity |
| - innermost circle ring | = dissolving the border to the deity |
| - second innermost circle ring | = contact with the deity |
| - second outermost circular ring | = perception of the deity |
| - outermost circular ring | = resolution to invoke the deity |

The four outer concentric circles are usually divided by four lines into four quarter circular rings each, so that the whole mandala is divided into four quarters. Each quarter corresponds to one of the four elements – so you can walk the path to the deity with the help of each of the four elements:

| | |
|---|---|
| - Fire: | with the help of courage, strength and determination |
| - Water: | with the help of compassion, devotion and love |
| - Air: | with the help of contemplation, recognition and affirmation |
| - Earth: | with the help of patience, growth and flourishing |

Which of these four ways one chooses for the invocation depends on one's own character. The tendency is to choose the element that appears most frequently in one's horoscope:

| | | |
|---|---|---|
| - Fire | (Aries, Leo, Sagittarius): | ecstasy |
| - Water | (Cancer, Scorpio, Pisces): | resonance |
| - Air | (Libra, Aquarius, Gemini): | clarity |
| - Earth | (Capricorn, Taurus, Virgo): | concentration |

You don't necessarily need a mandala for an invocation, but a mandala can help you better understand the steps of an invocation and your own style in an invocation.

The five circles in the mandala used here correspond to the five steps on the "Middle Pillar" from the Kabbalistic Tree of Life.

## VI 4. d)   The Gestures of the Deity

Some deities have special gestures and postures that one can use to identify with the deity in question. Since one assumes a posture typical of the deity with one's own body, this is one of the most powerful aids to imagination.

Such gestures and postures are for example:

- Shiva: lotus position
- Osiris: arms crossed in front of the chest
- Buddha: the various hand postures ("mudras")
- Innana: upper arms at a 45° angle down to the sides, forearms pointing straight up, palms forward
- Christ: cross posture
  etc.

Such typical postures and gestures are found in only a few deities.

# VI 5.   Music and Dance

## VI 5.   a) Music

A certain instrument is associated with some deities. It is therefore natural to play this instrument during the invocation of that deity.

| | |
|---|---|
| - Reed flute ("pan flute") | - Pan |
| - Flute | - Krishna, Athena |
| - Lyre | - Apollo |
| - Sistrum (a kind of rattle) | - Hathor, Bes |
| - harp | - Bragi, Dagda |
| - Vina, Sitar | - Saraswati |
| - drum, rattle | - Hanuman |
| etc. | |

There are also some compositions related to a particular deity, which can be played before the invocation if one wishes. This, of course, includes church and temple music in the broadest sense such as Christian chorales, Chinese praises of Kuan Yin, West African drum songs to the thunder god Shango, etc.

## VI 5. b)   Chanting

The singing of songs that have only a short text repeated over a long period of time is called "chanting." This form of chanting is a very effective method of building up tension and getting into concentration on a deity.

Especially when chanting is done in a group, it is a very effective way of both establishing contact with the deity to whom the song refers and entering into altered states of consciousness.

# VI 5. c)  Dance

Some deities such as the Indian Shiva, the Greek Pan, or the Egyptian Bes have also been associated with dance. These are usually ecstasy dances that originated in shamanism. Dervish dances from Islam also belong to this form of dance. Through such dances, concentration can be significantly increased.

Another form of magical-religious dance is the temple dance, through which a deity and his myths are represented. They stand between cult and show play and contain both pantomimic elements and elements of rhythmic ecstasy dance.

Since the temple dances usually require a longer training, they are usually not so well suited for an invocation. However, it is quite possible to simply use a handful of steps, postures and gestures from a Shiva temple dance in a Shiva invocation – this can be extremely powerful, even if it is not a full temple dance.

There are also some other dances that you might use in invocations such as sun dances, war dances, or ancestor dances.

It would probably be too much work and not very effective to learn such traditional dances especially for an invocation, but if one has already mastered such dances or knows elements from them, it is quite helpful to use them in invocations.

# VI 6.   The Structure of the Ritual

## VI 6. a)   The Dynamics

Each deity has its own character: Osiris is silent, Thor is choleric, Athena is warlike, Dagda is wise, Kuan Yin is kind, Orunmila knows the future, and so on. Therefore, one can also shape the dynamics of an invocation according to the character of the invoked deity. Of course, this requires some practice – in the beginning one should therefore limit oneself to the simple dynamics such as the more meditative character of Buddha and the more ecstatic character of Dionysus.

Probably, however, most people will initially choose the deity for invocation that is similar to their own character – therefore, the dynamics of the invocation will match the character of the invoked deity even without special planning.

## VI 6. b)   The Group Ritual

Performing an invocation together is very powerful when the participants are motivated and fully engaged, and perhaps have some practice.

One can distinguish between three fundamentally different forms of group invocation:

- Everyone invokes the deity in himself. In doing so, one supports each other by doing the same thing – a common "vibration" is created.

- All call the deity together into a person, who thereby receives a connection to this deity. In doing so, they all imagine that the selected person has the form of the deity.

These variants are found especially in initiations of all kinds and sometimes in magical healings.

- One priest or priestess invokes the deity into all persons that take part in the ritual. This is a widespread method in religious rituals.

## VI 6. c)   The Mythological Scenes

In invocations, scenes from the myths of the selected deity can also be imagined or represented. This can be done on one's own, thereby enhancing the power of the invocation.

However, one can also perform such a myth ritual as a group, in which case each person in the group imagines a different deity appearing in that mythe. Such a ritual then already approaches a mystery drama and an initiation ritual. By the fact that several deities from a myth are invoked at the same time, a field of tension arises, which does not arise by the invocation of a single deity. The initiation rituals of the Golden Dawn for example are based on this principle.

If one is practiced, one can also carry out such a multiple-invocation alone. Then one imagines all involved deities at their places in the room with their actions and takes the position of the central deity in the respective myth.


## VI 6. d)   Invocation and Evocation

These two methods are both invocations of a spirit of the dead or a deity. The only difference is into what place one invokes it: in an invocation into oneself, in an evocation to a place in front of oneself. So calling a deity into a statue is actually an evocation.

Evocations, however, have gotten a bad reputation because they have been a thorn in the side of missionaries. It used to be common practice around the world to go to a parent's grave in an emergency situation and call them over to ask for advice and help. This, of course, was a problem for the missionaries, because when people in general asked their dead parents and especially their dead father for help, they did not need the Christian God the Father: they had their own father in heaven and therefore did not need the abstract, general "father in heaven."

So the evocation of the dead parents ("evocation") was linked by the missionaries with all conceivable fears, in order to put people off evoking their dead parents. Thus, the dead father in the afterlife became the devil, the afterlife goddess the devil's grandmother, the burial chamber in the tumulus became hell ("cave"), the burial fire became hellfire, the dog as an afterlife companion became the hellhound, and so on.

Through this procedure, the missionaries finally achieved that the spirits of the dead and the invocation of the spirits of the dead ("necromancy", "evocations") became the creepiest thing of all for the people.

Today this method has a revivial in the form of family constellations.

37

# VI 7.  Variants

There are some variants of invocation, which refer only to the procedure:

- One stands and imagines the deity in front of oneself, then goes to the place where the deity stands and identifies with the deity.

- In India and Tibet, it is customary to imagine the deity (or guru) not in front of oneself, but above oneself.

- One stands and imagines the deity within oneself, whereby gradually the deity within oneself becomes clearly visible.

- The same can be done while sitting. When standing, the invocation is more of a ritual; when sitting, it is more of a meditation.

- One can sit or lie down comfortably and imagine the myths of the deity from the point of view of that deity, gradually taking on the form of the deity.

- The method just described is very similar to the dream journey already described, in which one's consciousness changes over to the deity.

- Finally there is the formless, improvised prayer to the deity or the conversation with the deity, by which one can approach the deity so far that one finally takes over the qualities of the deities and no longer experiences oneself as separate from the deity.

Of course, the variants described here cannot be strictly separated from each other – they are merely different starting points which overlap both in terms of their method and their experience. The separate listing of these variants only serves to make clear how one can approach the identification with a deity, i.e. its invocation.

One should always see which approach is most congenial to oneself and start with this approach and then continue to see how one might want to vary and supplement it the next time.

# VI 8.  Practice

As with many things, practice and repetition are extremely beneficial. Thus, the Golden Dawn writings say: "Invoke often!"

Invocations don't have to be hard, persistent work, either. It is probably easiest for many people to first make a dream journey to the deity and experience it directly in this way. Thus the deity becomes "alive" for oneself and becomes a part of one's life. You may also begin to dream about it. You can also ask the deity on dream journeys for healing, advice and help – if you then also receive advice and help, you no longer have to discipline yourself to regularly invoke the deity. If you need help, you will invoke the deity, for this works.

If one has invoked Pan and now has significantly more erotic adventures than before, one will probably invoke Pan of one's own accord more often and thereby get an ever more intimate contact with him.

Invocation is not an end in itself, but a tool – and if the tool clearly facilitates one's aspirations, one will use the tool again and again without thinking much about it. So the practice arises from the doing – and the doing arises from the desire for the fruits of that doing.

This form of practice arises completely casually. If in the past you always tried to drive a nail into the wall with your thumb and then you were shown what to do with a hammer, from then on you will always use a hammer when you want to drive a nail into the wall. You don't have to train yourself to remember the hammer when you want to hang a new picture on the wall of your room …

Likewise, once you have experienced thes magic-strengthening effect of an invocation, you will use it whenever you want to accomplish something in magic – simply because your magic becomes more effective that way.

Gradually, invocations will become something completely normal and almost everyday – one gets used to this state of identity with a deity. The invocations become simpler, easier and faster, until finally one only needs to awaken the image of the deity within oneself. This evocation of the image of the deity can be very quick and take only three or four seconds.

If one has carried out such a fast „second"-invocation effectively, one can have it checked by another person who is with one: If the „second"-invocation has been successful, one's own charisma changes very significantly. This is of course easier to notice with the somewhat wilder deities like Pan, Thor or Hekate than with the more mild deities like Isis, Apollo or Vishnu.

There is another way to check the effectiveness of an invocation, which comes from the Cypriot healer Daskalos: One imagines the deity, then invokes it into this imagination and then releases this imagination. If the image of the deity then remains anyway and possibly even starts to say or do something, the deity is actually present.

A similar state is achieved when one undertakes a dream journey to a deity and then finds that the deity says and does things that take one completely by surprise.

Both methods use the apparent momentum of the deity as evidence of its presence.

Especially when invoking one's own patron deity, it is quite likely that a love for that deity will gradually develop. This love is nothing romantic or turgid, but rather factual, deep and touching – like the emotional realization of a togetherness, a consubstantiality between oneself and the deity.

When feelings arise during the invocations, the invocations become much more effective. Thoughts grasp structures, but feelings set forces in motion. Therefore, love for a deity is the most effective way to invoke that deity.

If one invokes a deity often (or once invoked very intensively), with some probability the events from the myths of this deity will also occur in one's own life: One experiences the myths of the deity – live and with oneself as the main character.

Finally, there is a small point that relates to the actions of the deities in fulfilling wishes addressed to them. This area of invocations has, to my knowledge, been little explored.

A striking example is the god Pan. When asked for an erotic adventure, he always seems to use the same method: He makes another person dream intense erotic images that relate to the person who has invoked Pan. These dreams are so intense that the dreamer desperately wants to experience his dreams in reality and therefore tries to seduce the invoker.

Probably the other deities also have their special methods to realize a wish fulfillment.

## VI 9.  The Kundalini

There is another connection that is not immediately obvious. When one invokes a deity, one comes into contact with the realm in which there are qualities but no boundaries. The awakened Kundalini also has a quality, but is no longer limited by anything. Therefore, invocations and kundlini meditations may influence or stimulate each other. However, this is rarely evident.

Both processes (invocation and kundalini) are represented on the Kabbalistic Tree of Life by the "Serpent of Wisdom".

# VII  The Deity Consciousness

Little can be said about the experience of a successful invocation, that is the same for all invokers, since there are three influences that overlap during an invocation:

> - the horoscope and therefore the character of the invoker,

> - the contact of the invoker with the unbounded realm of the deities (on the Kabbalistic Tree of Life this is Da'ath),

> - the character of the invoked deity.

Of these three points, the second is the only point about which something general can be said.

The horoscope of the invoker shapes the experience of the invocation – a Taurus seeking the harmonious, pleasurable arrangement simply experiences this differently than a Scorpio seeking the intense tension.

A mischievous god of the wilderness and Eros like Pan is also naturally experienced quite differently than a venerable god of harmony and steady rhythm like the sun god Apollo.

Three things can be said about the second point, that is, about the demarcationless realm of deities:

> - The possibilities of perception become boundaryless, i.e. one can obtain all the information one wants to obtain during the identification with the deity by telepathy.

> - The possibilities of action are also unlimited – they depend only on the intensity of the identification with the deity. These possibilities of action also include such things as spontaneous healings, materializations and de-materializations – that is, "extraordinary magic".

> - The self-experience also changes during the duration of the identification with the deity: One also becomes without delimitation oneself. One no longer defines oneself by one's boundaries, but by one's quality. This is an extremely pleasant state, which one usually does not want to leave.

This boundaryless state is ultimately what will always draw you to invocations – simply because it feels so good.

This limitlessness is described by Buddha, among others, who says that an enlightened person has four limitless qualities:

- boundless equanimity (serenity – he sees everything as it is and accepts that it is now this way),

- boundless mercy (he helps everyone because he experiences all hardship as his own hardship),

- boundless love (because he has no more boundaries to other beings, he loves all beings like himself), and

- boundless joy (because of the lack of boundaries, he resonates together with everything – this „resonating together" is the cause and the essence of joy).

In most religions and myths, this state appears as the "place beyond the abyss," the "place where the gods dwell," and the like.

# VIII   The History of Invocation

Sometimes the history of a method makes the method itself a little clearer. Therefore, here follows a brief account of the development of invocation.

## VIII 1.   Paleolithic Age

The earliest evidence of invocation comes from the late Paleolithic period, about 40,000 years ago: the figure, carved from mammoth ivory, of a man with a panther head (usually thought to be the head of a lioness). Obviously, the hunters of that time wished to be able to hunt as fast and effectively as a panther.

This motif persisted until the early Neolithic period 12,000 years ago, where it can be found in the temples of Göbekli Tepe (northern Mesopotamia) as a stone panther-man totem pole, among others.

In the middle Neolithic period 7000 years ago, shamans appear as dancers dressed in panther skins on the murals of Çatal Höyük (Turkey).

In the epoch of royalty, which begins in Egypt around 3250 B.C., the shaman-priests wear either panther skins or lion skins – the lion replaced the panther when the jungle and savannah became steppe and desert.

Of course, the panther head and the panther skin can also be understood simply as an "image-adjective", which is supposed to characterize the hunter or shaman in question as "strong". The pictorial idea of being like a panther, however, comes so close to an invocation that there is little point in differentiating any further here.

In the late Paleolithic there are also representations of men with bull heads or with deer antlers. Since the herd animals are the symbols of fertility and procreative power worldwide (after all, they have so many young that they form herds), the bull men and the deer men will have invoked the procreative power of the herd animals.

# VIII 2.  Neolithic Age

Only three animal invocations are known from the Paleolithic: panther, bull, and stag. This tradition continued in the Neolithic period.

After the development of agriculture and animal husbandry around 8500 B.C., the grain god arose quite soon. It is based on the grain/man parable:

        sowing = procreation
        growth = life
        harvest = death
        storage = hereafter
        sowing = (re)birth

To this parable were added the seasons of the day and the seasons of the year as well as the directions of the sky (position of the sun during the day):

| sowing = begetting | = morning | = spring | = east |
|---|---|---|---|
| growth = life | = noon | = summer | = south |
| harvest = death | = evening | = autumn | = west |
| storage = beyond | = night | = winter | = north |
| sowing = (re)birth | = morning | = spring | = east |

From this complex parable, it appeared that the grain god had also been the death god. This motif is found among all agriculturalists from the Egyptians to the Aztecs.

In Egypt, this grain god and god of the dead was Osiris. He was depicted as a mummy, holding a flail in his right hand (agriculture: grain) and a shepherd's crook in his left hand (animal husbandry). Every Egyptian wanted to become after his death not only "like Osiris", but identical with Osiris – therefore e.g. an Egyptian with the name "Antef" called himself then "Osiris Antef" in the hereafter. This is equivalent to an invocation of Osiris on the afterlife journey.

There was also the widespread use of animal masks in the Neolithic period, which can then be found, among other things, in the epoch of kingship in Egypt, where, for example, the funeral priest always wears a mask of the jackal god Anubis. The wearing of a mask is a quite sure sign of an invocation.

# VIII 3.   Kingship

In the epoch of kingship, the mythology of the Neolithic period continued until the pharaoh Akhenaten formulated monotheism for the first time around 1350 BC.

The pharaoh as the representative of the sun god on earth was also the son of the sun god, thus the embodiment of the sun god – the pharaoh did not need to invoke the sun god, since the sun god resided already in the pharaoh since the coronation of the pharaoh. The coronation has been a form of invocation at that time.

Around 600 BC, from China to the Atlantic Ocean, it was taught that everyone is responsible for his own life. In order to come to this realization and to be able to implement it in everyday life, there were two methods: First, the afterlife journey of the shamans was developed into meditation, and second, the rituals of the shamans, through which they experienced astral travel and thus recognized their souls, were transformed into the Mysteries.

This new worldview emerged around 600 B.C. in many places at the same time:

> - in China by Lao-tse, Chuang-tse and Kungfu-tse,
> - in India by Patanjali, Buddha and Jaina,
> - in Persia by Zarathustra and the Mithras Mysteries,
> - in Egypt by the mysteries of Isis and Osiris,
> - in Greece by Pythagoras and the Mysteries of Eleusis,
> - in Thrace by Orpheus, Dionysus and the Mysteries of Samothrace,
> - in Rome by the mysteries of Liber Pater and Sol invictus,
> - among the Teutons by the initiation rituals of Tyr and Odin,
> - among the Celts through the Druid initiations,
>    etc.

Through these meditations and mysteries, many people at that time received a contact with their soul and with a deity. This is not yet a real invocation, but it comes quite close to it.

From about 800 A.D. the thought spread among Christians, in Islam and Judaism as well as in Hinduism that the soul of man must be a spark of the fire of the One God – among other things because otherwise it could not be eternal.

This thought led to the fact that one strove to become conscious of ons's soul and thereby also of a part of God. Further one strove in a second step to integrate one's own soul spark again into God's fire.

This two-part way to God is found with the Christian mystics, with the Sufis in

Islam, with the Kabbalists in Judaism, with the Yogis in Hinduism and in a slight modification also with the Mahasiddhis in Buddhism.

The first step of this path consists of taking responsibility for one's own life and meditating and possibly participating in mystery initiations. The second step of this path consisted mainly of love for the One God, through which one's own soul spark becomes a part of God's fire again.

Out of this striving and this love for God came the permanent invocation of God, the complete devotion to Him – be it God the Father, Christ, Allah, Yahweh, Krishna, Shiva, Vishnu, Buddha or yet another deity or even the Buddhist Nirvana.

The "magic-technical" roots of these invocations were the Paleolithic hunting spells, the Neolithic identification with the grain god, the bringing back of the spirits of the dead from the afterlife into their statue in this world by the shamans, and the invocation of a deity into their statue.

The mystics around 800 A.D. could thus fall back on a rich "magic-technical" tradition – although they will probably have known only a small part of this comprehensive invocation tradition at that time.

## VIII 4.  Materialism

In materialism (1500-1900 A.D.), which rejected all religion and magic, there were no more invocations as a conscious awareness technique. Invocations in this period were limited to imitation of models.

Alongside materialism, of course, religion continued to exist and at least preserved a memory of such possibilities as invocations – albeit in mysticism rather than in the mainstream of religion.


## VIII 5.  Globalization

In the present epoch of globalization, in which everything known up to now is put together into a new unity, also the invocation with all its different roots is newly discovered and explored – as in the present small booklet.

In this epoch both the magic-religious aspects and the psychological aspects are considered and integrated. But we are at present, however, still at the very beginning of this developement, since this new epoch has begun only about 80 years ago …

## English Books by Harry Eilenstein

- Living Magic (261 p.)
- The Synthesis of Physics and Magic (192 p.)
- Astral Projection for Beginners (60 p.)
- Invocations for Beginners (52 p.)
- Evocations for Beginners (62 p.)
- Auto-Movement for Beginners (60 p.)
- Elves for Beginners (56 p.)
  **These books will be puplished soon:**
- Telepathy for Beginners
- Telepathy for Advanced Learners
- Telekinesis for Beginners
- Life Force for Beginners
- Meditation for Beginners
- Kundalini for Beginners
- Hypnosis for Beginners
- Chakra-Magic for Beginners
- Astrology for Beginners
- Ritual Magic for Beginners

- Mandalas for Beginners
- Money Magic for Beginners
- Love Magic for Beginners
- Magic Research for Beginners
- Self-awareness for Beginners
- Symbolism of Numbers for Beginners
- Language of the Moon – for Beginners
- Magic Chant for Beginners
- Prophecy for Beginners
- Shamanism for Beginners
- Magic Objects for Beginners
- Da'ath-Magic for Beginners
- Crop Circles for Beginners
- Feng Shui for Beginners
- Magic for Beginners – Anthology I
- Magic for Beginners – Anthology II
- Magic for Beginners – Anthology III
- Magic for Beginners – Anthology IV

## Bücher von Harry Eilenstein

### Religion allgemein
- Die sieben Schritte des Lebens (428 S.)
- Muttergöttin und Schamanen (168 S.)
- Göbekli Tepe (472 S.)
- Die Göttin von Göbekli Tepe (144 S.)
- Totempfähle (440 S.)
- Christus (60 S.)
- Dakini (80 S.)
- Vajra (76 S.)

### Ägypten
- Hathor und Re 1:  Götter und Mythen im Alten Ägypten (432 S.)
- Hathor und Re 2:  Die altägyptische Religion – Ursprünge, Kult und Magie (396 S.)
- Isis (508 S.)

### Indogermanen
- Die Entwicklung der indogermanischen Religionen (700 S.)
- Wurzeln und Zweige der indogermanischen Religion (224 S.)

### Germanen
- Die Götter der Germanen (87 Bände – siehe nächste Seite)
- Odin (300 S.)

### Kelten
- Cernunnos (690 S.)
- Taliesin (228 S.)
- Der Kessel von Gundestrup (220 S.)
- Der Chiemsee-Kessel (76)

### Psychologie
- Über die Freude (100 S.)
- Das Geheimnis des inneren Friedens (252 S.)
- Das Beziehungsmandala (52 S.)
- Gefühle und ihre Verwandlungen (404 S.)
- einsgerichtet (140 S.)
- Liebe und Eigenständigkeit (216 S.)
- Von innerer Fülle zu äußerem Gedeihen (52 S.)

### Heilung
- Die Symbolik der Krankheiten (76 S.)

### Kunst
- Herz des Tanzes – Tanz des Herzens (160 S.)

### Drama
- König Athelstan (104 S.)

# Bücher von Harry Eilenstein

## „Magie für Anfänger"

- Telepathie für Anfänger (60 S.)
- Telepathie für Fortgeschrittene (52 S.)
- Telekinese für Anfänger (52 S.)
- Lebenskraft für Anfänger (60 S.)
- Meditation für Anfänger (56 S.)
- Kundalini für Anfänger (100 S.)
- Hypnose für Anfänger (56 S.)
- Auto-Movement für Anfänger (56 S.)
- Chakra-Magie für Anfänger (148 S.)
- Astralreisen für Anfänger (56 S.)
- Astrologie für Anfänger (120 S.)
- Ritual-Magie für Anfänger (56 S.)
- Mandalas für Anfänger (68 S.)
- Geldzauber für Anfänger (56 S.)
- Liebeszauber für Anfänger (52 S.)
- Invokationen für Anfänger (52 S.)
- Evokationen für Anfänger (60 S.)
- Elfen für Anfänger (56 S.)
- Magie-Forschung für Anfänger (140 S.)
- Selbsterkenntnis für Anfänger (52 S.)
- Zahlensymbolik für Anfänger (60 S.)
- Die Sprache des Mondes – für Anfänger (116 S.)
- Zaubergesänge für Anfänger (100 S.)
- Zukunftschau für Anfänger (60 S.)
- Schamanismus für Anfänger (52 S.)
- Magische Gegenstände für Anfänger (68 S.)
- Da'ath-Magie für Anfänger (64 S.)
- Kornkreise für Anfänger (348 S.)
- Feng Shui für Anfänger (96 S.)
- Magie für Anfänger – Sammelband I (696 S.)
- Magie für Anfänger – Sammelband II (664 S.)
- Magie für Anfänger – Sammelband III (580 S.)

## „Traumreisen"

- Traumreisen zu Heilpflanzen (700 S.)

## Magie

- Handbuch für Zauberlehrlinge (408 S.)
- Tarot (104 S.)
- Physik und Magie (184 S.)
- Die Synthese von Physik und Magie (200S.)
- Die Magie-Formel (156 S.)
- Krafttiere – Tiergöttinnen – Tiertänze (112 S.)
- Schwitzhütten (524 S.)
- Mythen und Magie der Harfe (116 S.)
- Magie heute – Berichte aus der Praxis (288 S.)

## Meditation

- Der Lebenskraftkörper (230 S.)
- Die Chakren (100 S.)
- Das Chakren-System mit den Nebenchakren (296 S.)
- Organe und Chakren (64 S.)
- Die platonischen Körper in den Chakren (156 S.)
- Meditation (140 S.)
- Drachenfeuer (124 S.)
- Kundalini I (676 S.)
- Reinkarnation (156 S.)
- einsgerichtet (140 S.)

## Astrologie

- Astrologie (496 S.)
- Photo-Astrologie (428 S.)
- Die astrologischen Aspekte (88 S.)
- Horoskop und Seele (120 S.)

## Kabbala

- Kursus der praktischen Kabbala (150 S.)
- Eltern der Erde (450 S.)
- Blüten des Lebensbaumes:
  - Die Struktur des kabbalistischen Lebensbaumes (370 S.)
  - Der kabbalistische Lebensbaum als Forschungshilfsmittel (580 S.)
  - Der kabbalistische Lebensbaum als spirituelle Landkarte (520 S.)

## Die Themen der 87 Bände der Reihe „Die Götter der Germanen"